THE
NON-TRAINER'S
GUIDE
TO
TRAINING

JOSÉ DELGADO FIGUEROA

THE
NON-TRAINER'S
GUIDE
TO
TRAINING

HISPANIC CARIBBEAN PRESS

HISPANIC CARIBBEAN PRESS
1720 Koulter Dr.
Columbia, SC 29210-7446
1 803 561 0957
sixcharacters@sc.rr.com

ISBN

Printed in the United States of America

TABLE OF CONTENTS

PREFACE

Let's say that:

- You are a skilled technician suddenly assigned to train fellow workers for customers; no time is available for educating you on instructional methods or delivery techniques.

- Due to financial strain, your small business or larger organization cannot afford the substantial fees that a trainer-development group would require.

- As a novice teacher of adults or an experienced post-secondary instructor, you are trying to strengthen your delivery skills. However, the few books on the subject are too expensive or too broad.

In such and similar cases, you can benefit from the contents of *The Non-Trainer's Guide to Training*. Rather than theory and research, this book attempts to focus on common-sense guidelines and recommendations, specific ideas, and useful reminders. The chapters in this guide group topics under eight major categories, presented in an informal, direct style. *The Non-Trainer's Guide to Training* has a specific focus: it aims to fill the gaps that lack of prior preparation has left in your skill set for delivering training. It assumes that your involvement in designing or developing the instructional program was minimal. In fact, this guide will be most beneficial to you if:

1. The organization sponsoring the training has conducted a thorough needs assessment. This assessment has included a job task analysis, with descriptions of expected performance of trainees on the job and a specification of mechanisms to evaluate performance against a clear standard. For example, a performance standard could be stated as: "Solder two wires permanently on the first attempt in less than a minute without waste."

2. You have been provided a complete statement of instructional objectives on which your materials are to be based. An instructional objective can be stated as: "Following a one-hour training session on soldering techniques, the trainee will be able to solder two wires permanently on the first attempt in less than a minute without waste."

3. A document that specifies the course-design is available for your inspection. The document should show the program's structure, as well as the sequence and scope of course topics.

4. The organization that sponsors the training has secured the services of a graphic artist or a specialist in graphic presentations.

5. You will be provided at least a basic set of instructional materials edited professionally for clarity, accuracy, style and mechanics, usability and presentation.

Following every section in *The Non-Trainer's Guide to Training* you will find a list of sources under the heading "If You Want to Learn More." The entries are listed in order of possible value to you, from most valuable to generally interesting.

If You Want to Learn More

1. Leslie Kelly, *The ASTD Handbook for Technical and Skills Training* (Alexandria, VA: American Society for Training and Development, 1994).

2. Leslie Kelly, *Supplement 1 to the ASTD Handbook for Technical and Skills Training* (Alexandria, VA: American Society for Training and Development, 2000).

3. Dugan Laird, *Approaches to Training and Development,* Third Edition Revised and Updated (New York: Basic Books, 2003).

4. Craig Schneier, Craig Russell, Richard Beatty, and Lloyd Baird, eds., *The Training and Development Sourcebook*, Second Edition (Amherst, MA: HRD Press, 1994).

5. Ora A. Spaid, *The Consummate Trainer: A Practitioner's Guide* (Englewood Cliffs, NJ: Prentice-Hall, 1986).

6. George M. Piskurich, *Training Development: Developing Training Courses Fast and Right* (San Francisco: Pfeiffer, 2009).

7. Robert F. Mager and Kenneth M. Beach, *Developing Vocational Instruction* (Belmont, CA: Pitman Learning Inc., 1987).

8. Angus Reynolds, *The Trainer's Dictionary* (Amherst, MA: HRD Press, 1993).

CHAPTER 1

WHY LEARN HOW TO DELIVER TRAINING?

The Beliefs
I believe that...

"I am an expert in my field, and that's all I require to teach other people my craft."

The Facts
But I'd be more efficient if I considered that...

I am an expert, so I am credible. That means that I am confident with the content, and people trust me to know what I am doing.

However, I have to learn to practice how to break down activities into steps, so I can show others how to do things in sequence. I also have to practice ways of communicating to others why I do what I do, when I do it, and how I do it. Moreover, I need to be able to communicate with adults in a way that shows I respect their own knowledge, experience and feelings, regardless of their origin, ethnic background, color, age, gender or sexual orientation.

15

The Beliefs
I believe that...

"When I lecture and make presentations, I am training. I make good presentations, so I am a good trainer."

The Facts
But I would be a more effective trainer if I considered that...

As part of training, sometimes I have to make presentations. Training implies that someone will be able to do something as a result of participation in an organized set of learning activities. Lectures and presentations are knowledge oriented; training is geared toward performance. Whereas lectures and presentations reach large numbers of people simultaneously, they do not ensure learning or acceptable performance. As a trainer, I need to tell trainees what I am going to do, then I need to do it, show

16

them how I did it, and have them practice doing it. Finally, I have to tell them how well they did it. The presentation only takes care of part of my training job.

The Beliefs

I believe that...

"Since I know the content inside out, I don't need to prepare too much for training in it."

The Facts

But I'd be a more effective trainer if I considered that...

I know the content inside out, and I need to make sure that I take into account the structure and sequence of the training experience. Because I know the content so well, it's easy for me to show trainees our final goal, but it's also easy for me to jump from one topic to another and soon lose my trainees in spite of my enthusiasm. To keep me from that, I need to plan training activities. I also have to make sure that trainees see me as a person who cares for the content and for them as adults trying to learn new skills. The best way for me to show the opposite is to jump into the training without previous planning, without knowledge of how to manage or conduct training, or without any idea of who the trainees are.

If You Want to Learn More

1. Malcolm M. Knowles, Elwood F. Holton III and Richard A. Swanson, *The Adult Learner*, Sixth Edition (Burlington, MA: Heinemann, 2011). Chapter One and Part Two.

2. Rosemary S. Caffarella, *Planning Programs for Adult Learners: A Practical Guide for Educators, Trainers and Staff Developers*, Second Edition (San Francisco: Jossey-Bass, 2010).

3. Ora A. Spaid, Chapter 3, "Not All Grown-ups Are Grown Up," in *The Consummate Trainer: A Practitioner's Perspective.* (Englewood Cliffs, NJ: Prentice-Hall, 1986).

4. Leslie Kelly, *The ASTD Handbook for Technical and Skills Training* (Alexandria, VA: American Society for Training and Development, 1994).

5. Allison Rossett, *Training Needs Assessment* (Englewood Cliffs, NJ: Educational Technology Publications, 1987).

6. Don Koberg and Jim Bagnall, *The Universal Traveler: A Soft-Systems Guide to: Creativity, Problem-Solving, and the Process of Reaching Goals* (Los Altos, CA: William Kaufmann, Inc., 2003).

7. Carol E. Kasworm, Amy D. Rose and Jovita M. Ross-Gordon, *Handbook of Adult and Continuing Education* (London: Sage Publications, 2010).

CHAPTER 2

BEFORE TRAINING BEINGS

Why bother to prepare to deliver training? Among the many messages you send out to your trainees when you don't prepare beforehand, you can include any or all of the following:

- I don't know what I'm doing.
- I don't care for you.
- I'd rather be somewhere else.
- I don't believe in this training program.
- You are not important.
- Your needs are not important.
- This training is not really that important.
- What you think of me is irrelevant to me.

Successful training depends on how well you organize the learning activities that allow trainees to test their level of performance as a result of training. As part of the training, you have to capture the trainees' attention and gain their commitment to learning new skills. The messages that you send out by being unprepared are the best way to lose both attention and any possibility of commitment.

Regardless of your level of content expertise, not preparing before training is a time-tested technique for failure.

Three Common Trainer Challenges—and How to Overcome Them

1 *Anxiety*—
prepare
notes that
you can fol-
low.

2. *Stage Fright*—
encourage participation:
it takes the focus
off you.

3. *Insecurity*—
master the content.

You need to consider both you and your trainees. Taking yourself as the primary source of directions for your learners, thoughtful prior preparation
helps you manage three common challenges to trainers: anxiety, stage fright, and insecurity.

Anxiety. This challenge may be related to the
seemingly overwhelming amount of things to keep
track of: content topics, participants' needs, equipment, handouts, schedules, manuals, physical facilities, online resources, manuals, etc.
To manage it: Prepare notes. Rather than at-
tempting to memorize what to do and say, use well-
organized notes. Don't write down full texts of content as if you were delivering a speech: outline main
points on which you can expand. Depending on your

setup, you can have those notes on your laptop screen or use sheet sizes big enough (8.5 x 11", 28.0 x 21.5 cm) to allow you to quickly glance at most of what you are doing in one session, rather than using note cards. Cards get out of order and have limited writing space.

Stage fright: Perhaps from lack of experience addressing a group or handling a particular topic, stage fright makes you over-prepare. You would probably surround yourself with notes by a speaker's stand, and depend on notes that keep you from looking at your participants.

To manage it: Reduce your role as the central figure in training. Stress trainee involvement. Remember that participants are human beings who need the training you are going to deliver. They have a job performance problem, and you are going to help them solve it. Build your preparation around allowing participants to interact and solve problems among themselves, with you as a guide who will facilitate development of skills. This way you remove the dependency that keeps you on the spotlight constantly.

Insecurity: From not knowing what participants will ask or whether they will be receptive.

To manage it: You must master the job, its procedures and processes, and the training materials. Then you should have answers to most questions. And if questions do come up that you can't answer, evaluate the inquiry before replying: Is this a relevant question? If it is, just prepare to respond, "I don't know, but I'll find out for you." (Then make sure you do find out or direct the person to someone or something that has the answer.) If it isn't relevant, you can answer, "I know that is important to

24

you, and although it is a different topic, we can pursue it privately later, if you are still interested."

The Setting

Taking participants as the primary focus while preparing to start training, you need to consider physical surroundings and the training environment.

Physical Surroundings

You should answer yes to the following, taking into account adult needs pertaining to all items:

- Does the room have adequate *lighting*?

Vision. Lighting in the room should allow everyone to see you and the visuals you use. You should be able to control the lights. If you are using screens, make sure that overhead lights do not shine directly on them. Keep in mind that dark rooms encourage drowsiness.

- Will all the participants be able to *hear*?

Hearing. Although you can control how well you project your voice and how loud everyone speaks during presentations, you can't very easily control background noise. Street noise can work against your training efforts; so can noise from halls and nearby rooms in the training building.

- Can you control the *temperature* in the room?

Temperature. When room temperature goes over about 72° F (24° C), trainers become sleepy.

When the temperature goes below 66° F (20° C), people become too cold and fail to concentrate well. You should be able to control room temperature or at least have access to someone who can control it when you need it changed.

• Is the training area *venti-lated* adequately?

Breathing. Participants tend to slow down when oxygen level decreases and cigarette smoke increases. If your facilities don't have windows, at least make sure that fans are working.

• Does each participant have a comforta*ble sitting* arrangement?

Comfort. This is particularly important in situations that require sitting down for long periods of time. Participants need enough elbow and knee room, about six square feet (5.4 m²) per trainee should be enough. If you are using desktop or laptop computers, make sure trainees have enough working space around them, especially if they are also using manuals and other hard-print materials. Keep chairs away from table legs. Whether chairs are upholstered and comfortable, remember that adults generally cannot sit for periods longer than 40 minutes in the same position.

• Are *bathroom* and *refreshment* areas nearby?

Hygiene. People need to know where they can purchase or receive refreshments during the training session, especially if you are not supplying them. As a consequence of refreshment and food consumption, they also need to know where the bathrooms are without having to ask.

Training Environment

Answer yes to the following. When setting up a training environment:

- Is *space* in the training area enough for the number of participants?

We tend to feel entrapped in rooms that are too small or whose ceilings are too low. Besides, if you plan to have trainees work in groups, they need enough space for it.

- Does the *shape* and *layout* of the room allow for a seating arrangement free of distractions? Can all participants see from any part of the room?

Shape and layout of the room influence how much and how good interaction can be between you and trainees, and among trainees. (See suggested layouts on page 32.)

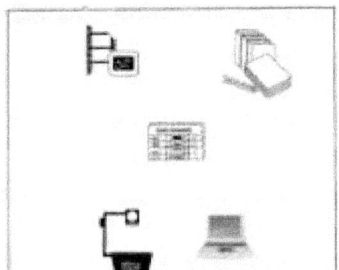

Participants should be able to see each other. The way chairs and tables are arranged depends on the number of participants and the type of interaction you expect among them. However, the worst possible arrangement is classroom style, with tables and

27

chairs parallel to each other. For groups over 20, consider grouping trainees in round tables. For groups of about 10 to 20, you may shape tables into a "U." You can locate your own table at the top of the opening on the "U." (If you are using several tables, make sure that none of the participants is forced to sit behind a column.) For smaller groups, a single table may be adequate.

Suggested sitting arrangements in the training room.

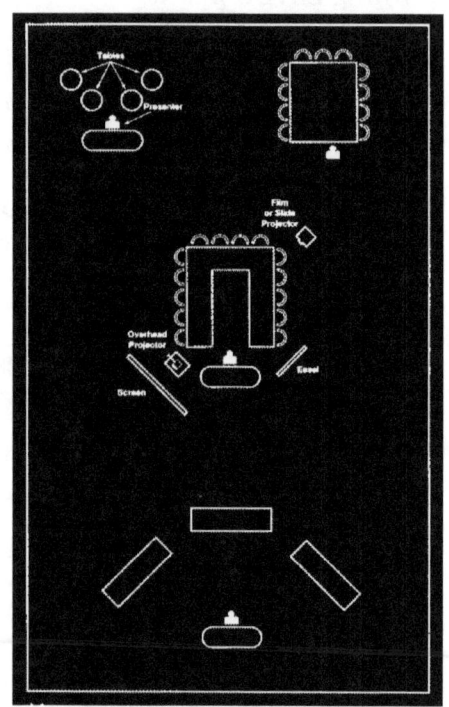

• Is adequate *equipment* available?

Besides chairs, tables and your own desk or workstation, equipment needs to vary with the type of training strategies you use. Whether you need a projector, a videotape or compact-disc player, a computer monitor or an easel pad, everything you dis-
28

play has to be visible to everyone in the room from all areas. Test all electrical equipment before the session begins, including laptop batteries, and secure spare bulbs for projectors. If you must secure equipment from a central location or department in the organization, the person in charge should be available while training is in progress. If you have to use props, such as equipment for demonstrations and simulations, set them up and make sure they are ready to work as expected before you need to use them. When using computer technology to illustrate concepts for practice, verify that your examples are loaded up and operate under the application version available on the system you are using. Some vendors won't allow you to open a file developed under an older release of their software.

- Are *all necessary materials and supplies* available in the training area?

It is extremely important that everything you need to be in the training area before the training session begins. This prevents you from having to run in and out of the training area to get tools you forgot. Before training starts, prepare a checklist of the materials and supplies you will need, and where you can get them. Also keep handy the contact number of a person in the organization who can run errands for you if you happen to overlook something. Supplies you need vary with the techniques and tools you use in training. Generally, you will need markers for the easel pad and the white board, chalk if you are using a chalk board, acetate (for on-the-spot transparencies) wax pencils, writing pads, pencils, and a pencil sharpener. You may also need computer diskettes to save work completed in training. Materials for you may include sets of slides, charts, films, trainer guides, computer disks, and notes. For trainees, you may need handouts, manuals, job aids, and props. All materials that trainees need must be set out, organized, and available to them. Put materials as individual packets on tables, one per seat.

Two Equations You Must Acknowledge

```
1.  Knowing Your Subject =
    Building Confidence
```

Whether you are a professional trainer or a subject-matter expert doing training, knowing your subject is your greatest source of confidence for yourself and for trainees.

When you master your subject, you are able to focus on training strategies and techniques, instead of concentrating on the accuracy of your statements.

As a well-informed trainer, you know that you can handle questions from the group, and you are in a better position to ask the kinds of questions that promote thought and discussion.

In terms of your image as a training facilitator, your mastery of the subject becomes obvious to participants early on. This lends you credibility and makes participants more confident that they are really learning useful, appropriate skills.

```
2.  Knowing Your Trainees =
    Meeting Their Needs
```

Make an effort to know the demographic characteristics of your trainees prior to the beginning of the training program. Who are your trainees?

What's their age bracket? What positions do they hold in the organization? How long have they been with the organization? What experience do they have in the field for which you are training? Do they know why they are going through training? Does any of them have special needs due to language or a physical challenge? Are any of them foreign nationals with special cultural needs?

To collect information, the organization itself may already have questionnaires, or you may have to design one. These questionnaires should be part of whatever pre-course materials you send out to potential trainees. You should get them back before doing any final planning for training delivery. Clearly, once training itself begins, trainees will be able to introduce themselves; however, you need to get personal and professional information about them beforehand for several reasons, among them:

- You can adjust your materials' vocabulary and technical level to your trainees' level and potential learning styles (for example, verbal or graphic-oriented, detailed or summarized). When you talk over their heads, you lose them; when you talk down to them, they become resentful.

- You can find out whom you already have in the room to the age group and professional background of your trainees. Your examples, for instance, can come from fields of common knowledge and interest to your trainees. From background information you can also get a general idea of what kinds of individual or group training activities will or will not work for groups with certain demographic profiles.

31

If You Want to Know More

1. Jane C. Zahn, "Differences Between Adults and Youth Affecting Learning," *Adult Education*, Vol. 17, No. 2, 1967, pp. 67-77.

2. William J. Rothwell, *Adult Learning Basics* (Alexandria, VA: American Society for Training and Development, 2008).

3. Rosemary S. Caffarella, *Planning Programs for Adult Learners: A Practical Guide for Educators, Trainers, and Staff Developers*, Second Edition (San Francisco: Jossey-Bass, 2008).

4. Sharon B. Merriam, Rosemary S. Caffarella, Lisa M. Baumgartner, *Learning in Adulthood: A Comprehensive* Guide (San Francisco: Jossey-Bass, 2006).

5. Larry N. Davis and Earl McCallon, *Planning, Conducting, Evaluating Workshops* (Austin, TX: Learning Concepts, 1974).

6. Dugan Laird, Chapter 12, "What Should Training Rooms Be Like?" in *Approaches to Training and Development* (Reading, MA: Addison-Wesley Publishing Co., 1985).

7. Lawrence Munson, Chapter 7, "Choosing the Seminar Setting," in *How to Conduct Training Seminars* (New York, NY: McGraw-Hill, 1984).

8. Robert W. Bailey, Chapter 4, "Sensing-Vision" and Chapter 22, "Physical and Social

Environments," in *Human Performance Engineering: A Guide for System Designers* (Englewood Cliffs, NJ: Prentice Hall, 1982).

9. Paul Barber, Chapter 5, "Mental Workload, Attention and Performance," in *Applied Cognitive Psychology: An Information-Processing Framework* (London and New York: Methuen, 1988).

10. Barry H. Kantowitz and Robert D. Sorkin, Chapter 17, "Microenvironments," in *Human Factors: Understanding People-Systems Relationships* (New York, NY: John Wiley & Sons, 1983).

11. Edward T. Hall, Chapter III, "The Biochemistry of Crowding," and Chapter X, "Distances in Man," in *The Hidden Dimension* (Garden City, NY: Doubleday Anchor Books, 1966).

12. Robert G. Owens, Chapter Four, "Motivation," in *Organizational Behavior in Education*, Tenth Edition (Englewood Cliffs, NJ: Prentice-Hall, 2010).

CHAPTER 3

TIME TO BEGIN
THE TRAINING PROGRAM

Your training program may include pre-course packets that you send out to potential participants. It may also include welcome or hospitality sessions the night before the official start of the program, or other means to get acquainted. However, it's when you all meet in the same room at a pre-set time that training begins. Right there and then.

To begin the training program you should follow a routine. This means that the process involved in the routine should be the same across training groups; the content of the routine itself, however, should vary with the group profile. Because it is a routine, it consists of steps to follow. It also involves motivational aspects that you have to consider throughout the training program. Underlying it all, keep in mind your goals and the program's objectives.

Your Goals

As a training facilitator, activities that you hold as you begin training should:

- Make trainees feel welcome.

- Inform trainees what the training program is and what it helps them accomplish.

- Help you become aware of trainee expectations, and allow you to let trainees know which ones they can expect to fulfill.

- Set ground rules.

- Ensure that trainees begin to see your role as facilitator of learning rather than as the total expert.

Before Trainees Come In

Be in the training room at least one hour before the training session is scheduled to start. You want to make last minute checks on supplies, especially materials for nameplates, such as card stock and markers. You also need to check materials and the room's layout. Additionally, you want to be there to greet participants as they arrive. On a board or flip chart, and written in letter size that is legible to all participants in the room, you should have stated:

- Training program title
- Trainer's name
- Starting time

Introducing Participants and the Training Program

As trainees arrive and you get into preliminary activities:

1. Greet trainees. Most of the time this is your first opportunity to make a personal statement regarding your concern for trainees. Promptly at the scheduled starting time, greet and welcome assembled participants, and state your name and position in the organization you represent.

2. Direct the participants' attention to the nameplate material in front of them. If you have determined previously where participants will sit, and have prepared nameplates beforehand, this should have been obvious to trainees as they walked into the room. Otherwise, see the sidebar on the following page, "What's in a Name?"

3. Explain the purpose of the training program. Do so in terms that would answer the trainees' question, "Why are we here?"

4. Describe broadly the resources available to reach the training goal. Through this description, you are trying to tell trainees how they are going to accomplish the purpose of training. Include general information on training length, materials, and activities that you will be holding.

5. Introduce yourself as the trainer, including relevant information about yourself. The purpose here is to let trainees know why (on what authority) you are addressing them.

6. Request that trainees introduce themselves. If you wish, guide them with a transparency or flip chart sheet with specific questions: who they are, where they live, for whom they work, what their job title, what they do, and why they are in the training program. You may use alternatives to this introduction method (see "If You Want to Learn More" at the end of this section).

What's in a Name?

We think of our name as one of our most distinctive features, and value other people's recognition of it as representative of our own selves. This probably accounts for expressions such as: "He dragged my good name through the mud," or "I'll do it or my name isn't..." In a training environment it does make a different when the trainer shows interest in pointing out trainees' names and making sure that everyone gets to know everyone else.

With that purpose in mind, the decision to issue name tags may be a matter of trainer taste or institutional policy. If participants are expected to interact in ways that allow them to be within three feet (1 meter) of each other, experience alone tells us that name tags are enough.

For most training room arrangements, use nameplates that participants can place in front of them and that most other people in the room can read from their own seats. This allows you to call on individuals by the name they prefer to be called, without a special effort to memorize everyone's name. Nameplates can be made of a neutral, non-gloss 8.5" x 11" (28.0 x 21.5 cm) sheet of construction paper or card stock, folded once vertically. Just make markers available for trainees, and instruct them to use letters big enough for you to see from the front of the room.

7. Request that trainees volunteer their expectations from training, and record them on a flip chart, board, or transparency that all participants can see. (You may have solicited this information already during introductions; if you have, make sure you write it down as the information is offered.) When a participant says that he/she does not know what to expect, state that it is alright not to know—but you must allow the trainee to express that. The purpose of this step is to find out unexpressed agenda items that you may or may not be able to help trainees meet through the training program. Allow all expectations to surface and write them down without judging their validity. Your attitude

of acceptance for the trainees' response also builds on their trust for you. Remember that at this point trainees may begin to see you as genuinely interested in their needs and as a non-threatening facilitator of learning. They can just as easily see you as someone who says one thing and does something completely different, thereby nipping any budding commitment from trainees.

8. Review expectations and relate them to a list of topics preset for training. Show trainees that the training program consists of a logical sequence of topics, but also that you are flexible to accommodate particular needs and interests of the group through special sessions, or by referring trainees to other sources of information. You can also point out which expectations cannot be met, because they are unrelated to the training program, or because of their scope. Showing concern for legitimate trainee expectations is important. It is equally crucial that trainees understand the limits of the training program. Save the list of expectations, or post it in a visible place in the room, as a reminder to you and to participants. At the end of the training program you can go back and compare which of the trainees' expectations were met as envisioned from the start.

9. Present the training program overview. Present the final goals of each major component, in terms of what the trainee will be capable of doing by completing activities under each major component.

10. Restate your awareness of trainee expectations, and state your own expectations of trainees. The purpose of this step is to set ground rules. It also helps trainees raise questions about the training process, if they have any.

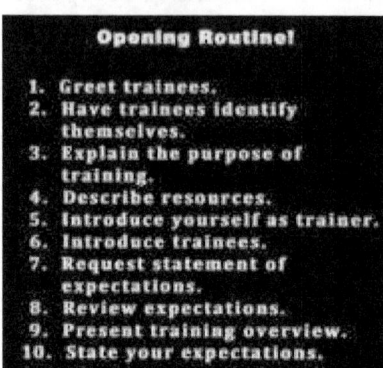

Opening Routine!

1. Greet trainees.
2. Have trainees identify themselves.
3. Explain the purpose of training.
4. Describe resources.
5. Introduce yourself as trainer.
6. Introduce trainees.
7. Request statement of expectations.
8. Review expectations.
9. Present training overview.
10. State your expectations.

Explain the schedule; call attention to coffee and lunch breaks, beginning and ending time each day, and special homework assignments. This may also be a good time to explain how you will handle questions during presentations and demonstrations. (Do you welcome them at any point, or do you prefer that trainees hold their questions until you are done?) Describe attendance expectations, where trainees can receive messages, and whom to see about special requests.

Now Is the Time to Develop Motivation

From the moment you step into the training room you have to remind yourself that motivation is a key factor in training efforts. You may find out from listening to trainee expectations that among them may be individuals who came because they were told to do so, or people who thought they knew why they were there. Most of the time, willing, unwilling, and even confused trainees will have to be in training for the length of the program. You may not be able to help all, nor may all want to be helped. Keep telling yourself that your trainees are all adult

42

and know how to bear the consequences of their choices.

However, your responsibility also remains to try to keep trainees interested and motivated enough that they will develop a personal commitment to making the best possible use of the training opportunity.

To keep participants interested:

- Be human: smile, use humor, be active, address by name, keep eye contact.

- Make topics matter: don't digress or ramble into irrelevant subjects.

- Watch your pace.

- Encourage participation. Get your trainees involved in training activities. You can achieve this by asking participants to volunteer information, by allowing them (within reason) to relate relevant anecdotes or success stories, and by breaking them up into working teams.

As adults we need to feel that we are part of the learning process. Getting trainees involved recognizes that they do bring valuable experiences into the learning environment, and that you acknowledge their importance. This helps build self-confidence and commitment to completing program activities.

When trainees begin to look as if their attention were decreasing, provided that it is not due to an environmental deficiency, it may be due to a feeling of lack of involvement. You will notice that talking faster or louder will irritate trainees, but will not

increase their level of interest if they are not participating actively.

Show that you are human. This does not mean
that you can break down and cry when you hear sad
stories. It does imply that you should:

- Address participants by name. This recognizes them as individuals. It also shows
  them you are concerned about them as human beings.

- Keep eye contact. If you have trouble with
  this and have been advised to stare at
  points in the back of a room instead of looking at anyone in the eye, you may continue
  to do this. However, at least every so often
  refocus the point where you look in the
  back. Presenters tend to be static and mo-
  notonous when they seem to be staring into
  space all the time, getting directions from
  an invisible being. Better yet, look at participants. Besides serving as a gauge regarding interest in the presentation, eye contact
  helps to keep trainees alert and gives them
  the feeling that you are looking at them as
  individuals. If you can't bring yourself to
  look at people in the eye, at least focus on
  the bridge of their noses, but make an attempt to look at people's faces. On the other
  hand, staring or glaring will make trainees
  uncomfortable; therefore, don't focus on one
  individual for long periods of time.

- Smile when appropriate. High intensity
  faces spill over into the general feeling in a

training room. Get in the habit of internally analyzing your own face for tension, stress or frowns while you facilitate training. As the day wears on, so does our countenance.

- Use humor when appropriate. Be careful , however, to consider the group's profile before you tell a joke or anecdote or make humorous comparisons. Telling jokes whose butt is an ethnic group, a gender, a sexual orientation or a physical challenge is in poor taste and insensitive. Furthermore, you are likely to offend someone in your group, with a subsequent loss in credibility, interest and commitment.

- Be active. Holding on to a lectern or always standing behind your desk in front makes you the focus of a spiraling wheel, much like the one hypnotists use. Add a low tone of voice and soon you will have a very sedate group of uninterested people.

- Remind trainees of why topics matter to them. Your trainees will soon tune you out if they don't feel that what you are telling them is important to them. The content of a presentation and the process of any training activity have to be related to training goals. If you feel that such a connection is difficult to establish, make sure that you state the interrelationship of topics and activities, and why they are relevant.

- Watch your pace. We have all had a teacher who habitually finished covering the material in a textbook and forgot to tell the students. Training, however, is trainee-oriented: your pace must be tuned to your trainees, within reason. Pace, actually, is not related to speed only. It also has to do with changes in approach. Because your program is trainee-centered, you need to keep an eye out for those who may be falling behind, and provide them assistance or suggest alternate ways to reach the same training goal.

To Commitment by Maintaining Interest

So now that you have their interest, how do you get to commitment? The hypothetical questions that follow will help you plan strategies for retaining the interest of your trainees on the basis of their needs as adults. You will find that developing trainee commitment to your program depends on how well you recognize the following trainee concerns as important.

Trainees will ask:

- *Why* am I learning this?

Keep in mind the experience and skills they bring to the training environment, and avoid redundancy. Make training goals and performance objectives clear.

- *How* does this relate to me?

Relate training activities to the professional and job performance goals of trainees. Education focuses on information; training focuses on specific job activities and how to complete them.

- What do I already know that helps me master this new skill?

Use strategies and techniques that help people transfer what they already know into what they are now learning to do. Remind them of activities they already perform, and look for points of contact between the known and the new behavior they have to learn.

- May I try it out *myself?*

Use techniques that allow trainees to apply significant chunks of theory immediately after it is presented and demonstrated.

- *What* will I be able to do as a result of this?

Inform trainees of what they are going to be able to do if they successfully complete the training program. State their final behavior in terms of what they will be able to see themselves doing if they master training skills.

- *How* am I doing?

Provide trainees immediate feedback. After significant components in the training program, allow trainees to test their level of mastery of skills by completing application or demonstration exercises. When the level of mastery is inadequate, suggest or prescribe actions to remedy deficiencies. In each case, focus on the skill the trainee is testing and be positive (especially when the trainee has made several attempts) while stressing the need to improve. For instance, instead of saying, "You are proficient at this, but you are not doing this one right," try,

"You are proficient at this, <u>and</u> to get to the same level with this one, you can..,"

- *What's* next?

Provide spiral learning activities: in training, each activity should address a subset of skills upon which you build increasingly broader concepts. Maintain trainee focus on what they have accomplished and where they are headed. To accomplish this use road maps to indicate starting points, milestones and final goal. Trainees should be able to see such progress charts at appropriate times, such as at the end of each significant training segment.

If You Want to Learn More

1. Ora A. Spaid, Chapter 1, "What Seems to Work," and Chapter 9, "Learning from Learning" in *The Consummate Trainer: A Practitioner's Perspective* ((Englewood Cliffs, NJ: Prentice-Hall, 1986).

2. Barry H. Kantowitz and Robert D. Sorkin, Chapter 7, "Human Information Processing," in *Human Factors: Understanding People-Systems Relationships* (New York: John Wiley & Sons, 1983).

3. John M. Keller, "Strategies for Stimulating the Motivation to Learn," *Performance and Instruction*, October 1987, pp. 1-7.

4. William J. Rothwell, *Adult Learning Basics* (Alexandria, VA: American Society for Training and Development, 2008).

5. Malcolm M. Knowles, Elwood F. Holton, III, Richard A. Swanson, *The Adult Learner*, Seventh Edition (Burlington, MA: Betterworth-Heinemann, 2011).

6. Raymond J. Wlodkowski, *Enhancing Adult Motivation to Learn: A Comprehensive Guide for Teaching All Adults* (San Francisco: Jossey-Bass, 2007).

7. Robert Marzano, *Classroom Management That Works: Research-based Strategies for Every Teacher* (Alexandria, VA: Association for Supervision and Curriculum Development, 2008).

8. James L. Adams, Chapter 2, "Perceptual Blocks," Chapter 4, "Cultural and Environmental Blocks," in *Conceptual Blockbusting: A Guide to Better Ideas*, Second Edition (New York: W. W. Norton, 1979).

9. Carol E. Kasworm, Amy D. Rose and Jovita M. Ross-Gordon, *Handbook of Adult and Continuing Education* (London: Sage, 2010).

10. John W. Newstrom and Edward Scannell, *Games Trainers Play* (New York: McGraw-Hill, 1980); *More Games Trainers Play* (New York: McGraw-Hill, 1983).

11. Steven A. Beebe, Timothy F. Mottet and K. David Roach, *Training and Development: Enhancing Communication and Leadership Skills* (Boston: Pearson, 2012).

12. Doni Tamblyn and Sharyn Weiss, *The Big Book of Humorous Training Games* (New York: McGraw-Hill, 2000).

CHAPTER 4

WHICH TRAINING METHOD TO USE?

Aside from consideration about training tools and facilities, you may be in charge of deciding which method and techniques to use to conduct training. If this is the case, consider the features of different training methods before you choose one or another, or a combination of all. What guidelines do you have for selecting methods and techniques? Most often training programs suggest or prescribe that trainees demonstrate the ability to perform under one or more of the following categories:

- Discrimination: Focuses on the skill of knowing when to perform a given action.

- Problem solving: Stresses processes for working through possible solutions to a problem.

- Recall: Verifies that the learner has committed information, such as steps in a procedure, to memory.

- Manipulation: Entails using or operating objects or instruments, such as a control panel or a laboratory device.

- Speech: Requires the learner to speak about a subject or to describe a process.

During the process of needs analysis, a training specialist in your organization has to identify the type of performance involved in the task or group of tasks (job) for which you are conducting training. You can then select the instructional method and the techniques that best support the trainees' performance goal.

Five common training methods include presentations, structured discussion, demonstration and performance, and laboratory or problem solving.

Presentations

Presentations focus entirely on the trainer, who has complete responsibility for presenting the material. The trainer may use audiovisual aids to support the verbal message.

Use presentations if you want:

- Primarily one-way communication.
- Constant student attention.
- To save time.
- Passive trainees.
- To address a large group.
- Complete control of the information flow.

Avoid presentations when you want:
- Interaction among participants.
- To maintain trainee attention.
- To help trainees retain information.

Structured Discussion

Structured discussion consists of assigning topics to probe or tasks to complete following specific guidelines for how to proceed within time constraints. Structured discussion allows trainees to play an active role in the training process. It helps

54

participants acknowledge the experience that they bring to the training environment and use this experience for building new knowledge. Communication in structured discussion goes in many directions. Structured discussion can take place with the whole group, or through small teams that gather to consider specific topics or problems and then report to the group as a whole. The trainer's main role is asking probing questions and promoting productivity, posing problems, and managing participation of trainees.

Use structured discussion when you want to:

- Keep trainee interest and participation at a high level.
- Maintain an informal atmosphere.
- Provide sufficient opportunities for feedback.
- Motivate through involvement.

Avoid structured discussion if you:

- Don't have enough time.
- Feel that trainees could get out of control.
- Need to develop your own skills in group leadership.

Demonstration and Performance

Demonstration and performance puts the trainer in the role of demonstrator. You explain and show the actions that the trainee must perform to complete a task. This method allows the trainee to learn by doing, while you stand ready to provide guidance, correct errors and suggest ways to improve performance.

Use demonstration and performance when you want to:

- Increase chances of retention of training.
- Reinforce a concept by presenting it in different attention-getting devices.
- Build trainee confidence.

Avoid demonstration and performance when you:

- Don't have enough time for a clear and thorough demonstration.
- Can't allow all trainees enough time to attempt performance with opportunities for trial and error.
- Can't refrain yourself from making startling or unkind remarks about trainee performance.

Laboratory or Problem Solving

Either laboratory or problem solving, or both used in combination, give participants the opportunity to apply knowledge in solving problems similar to those on the job. Trainees receive guidelines for what they are to do, and then are allowed to proceed on their own or as members of work teams. The trainer provides guidance as requested.

Use laboratory or problem solving when you want:
- To afford learners opportunities to test the validity of information.
- To simulate real life situations, without wasting on-the-job resources.
- Total trainee involvement.

Avoid laboratory or problem solving when you:

- Can't provide equipment and time for all train-ees to complete exercises or other related activities.
- Are limited by logistics: laboratory work in-creases management requirements for the trainer.
- Feel that trainees are inadequately prepared to handle application activities due to lack of knowledge or enough comprehension of the task or process.

What Difference Does It Make?

When you choose a method (or a combination of them: they are not mutually exclusive), remember that trainees are usually able to retain a great deal more of information when they are personally in-volved in the learning activity. Very little of what trainees read or hear during training remains with them a few days after the training session—usually about 10% a week later. However, if they are able to describe what they are doing as they are doing it, they increase the chances of retaining information and achieving a deeper understanding of job tasks.

Practice does improve performance, and you need to be realistic about what skills trainees must be able to demonstrate within the framework of re-sources available, especially time and equipment. Getting trainees involved from the start can help you stretch those resources and the benefits to both them and your organization.

If You Want to Learn More

1. William J. Rothwell, *Adult learning Basics* (Alexandria, VA: American Society for Training and Development, 2008.

2. Malcolm M. Knowles, Elwood F. Holton, III, Richard A. Swanson, *The Adult Learner,* Seventh Edition (Burlington, MA: Betterworth-Heinemann, 2011).

3. Raymond J. Wlodkowsky, *Enhancing Adult Motivation to Learn: A Comprehensive Guide for Teaching All Adults*, Third Edition (San Francisco: Jossey-Bass, 2007).

4. Sharon B. Merriam Rosemary S. Caffarella and Lisa M. Baumgartner, *Learning in Adulthood: A Comprehensive Guide* (San Francisco: Jossey-Bass, 2007).

5. Jon Saphier, Mary Ann Haley-Speca and Robert Gower, *The Skillful Teacher: Building Your Teaching Skills,* Sixth Edition (Acton, MA: Research for Better Teaching, 2008).

6. Dugan Laird, Chapter 9, "How Do People Learn," and Chapter 10, "What Methods Shall I Use?" in *Approaches to Training and Development*, Second Edition (Reading, MA: Addison-Wesley Publishing Co., 1985).

7. Lawrence Munson, Chapter 1, "The Growing Importance of Training Seminars: Training Vehicles," in *How to Conduct Training Seminars* (New York: McGraw-Hill, 1992).

8. Robert W. Bailey, Chapter 7, "Perception, Problem Solving and Decision Making," in *Human Performance Engineering: A Guide to System Designers* (Englewood Cliffs, NJ: Prentice-Hall, 1982).

9. Alan Jay Zaremba, *Organizational Communication*, Sixth Edition (New York: Oxford University Press, 2009).

10. James L. Adams, Part One—"Thinking," in *The Care and Feeding of Ideas* (Lexington, MA: Addison-Wesley Publishing Co., 1986).

11. Frank E. Saal and Patrick A. Knight, Chapter 7, "Personnel Training: Training Techniques, Methods, and Procedures," in *Industrial/Organizational Psychology: Science & Practice* (Pacific Grove, CA: Brooks/Cole Publishing Co., 1990).

CHAPTER 5

THE TRAINER AS PRESENTER

You, the Public Speaker

The presenter is one of the roles you will most likely play in the training process. You may have to present information with varying degrees of trainee involvement, when trainees need a background before they can try a skill on their own. You may also need to make a presentation to reinforce concepts and to summarize a major component.

Because you are presenting to trainees, you have to be aware of your skills as a presenter in a training context. You also have to keep in mind how you are going to interact with trainees. Public speakers have to handle their delivery appropriately and manage possible interruptions during delivery.

Delivery. When you are addressing the group:

DO

DON'T

DO	DON'T
Project your voice. This is not equivalent to yelling. It means that you are making an attempt to have people hear you, even if they are in the last row. If you don't know for sure, ask them whether they can hear you.	Yell until your voice is hoarse. You will ruin your voice and irritate listeners.

DO	DON'T
Enunciate correctly. Be more aware of mouth movement and pronounce words as if your English teacher were among trainees.	Over-pronounce words. It makes you look silly, unless you are on stage and your trainees are dispersed in a stadium.
Choose your words according to your trainees' age, professional and cultural background. If knowing specialized terms is part of the training, explain them as you use them.	Use technical jargon or acronyms that trainees cannot understand. Do not assume trainees know what the acronym stands for. You are not impressing anyone: you are confusing people who may not dare ask what you are talking about because they fear ridicule, not because they understand what you are saying.
Pace yourself as you speak, so that you can control your speed.	Rush through your presentation. It makes for slurred sounds, not words.
Face trainees when you speak. If you have to write on a flip chart or	Talk to the board or flip chart or while facing windows. When you talk

64

board, wait until you are done writing before addressing the group again or write with your body and face at least partially turned toward trainees.

against the board your voice becomes dull; trainees usually have trouble hearing muffled sounds uttered against a flat surface. It is an annoying habit and ruins your chances for rapport with trainees.

Vary the tone of your voice, emphasizing important points when possible and raising your tone of voice.

Speak in a monotone. It makes people sleepy and ruins trainee interest, especially in the afternoon, following lunch

Stand erect when you speak. Allow for informal moments when you may find it relaxing to sit on your desk or to create an informal atmosphere for group discussion, but try to keep your posture while you address the group.

Stand against walls or pillars as if you were holding them up, or bend your leg back against the wall.

Use gestures that reinforce ideas you are expressing in your presentation. For example, you can use your fingers to count three or four important concepts as you present them. Certain hand motions also help convey certain mean-

Bat your hands around as if you couldn't control them. Try to keep your hands below shoulder level, unless the point you are making requires that you use your hands otherwise. Avoid stretching as if tired or bored while you are in

ings, such as making a circulating movement with your hand when you talk about progress, or moving your hands from one side to another as you refer to process of change.	front of the group.
Move around and about the room, keeping in mind that your trainees should be able to see you at all times. Keep eye contact with participants.	Stand for prolonged periods of time behind trainees or on the same spot. Avoid staring at any person for too long.

They Who Interrupt You

Interruptions break trainee concentration on your presentation. It also undermines the effectiveness of your presentation. Unfortunately, interruptions are practically unavoidable, and in training generally come in four forms: latecomers, messages, mobile devices and challenging personalities. Fortunately, they can be managed.

Latecomers. When someone comes in late, greet the person, wait until the person has found a seat, and provide a quick summary of what you have been doing up to that point. How much you defer to latecomers is proportional to their lateness: the later they are, the less of a chance you have to bring them up to date.

Messages. Explain that no messages will be given to trainees unless it is an emergency. This prevents the usual parade of receptionists and telephone operators from invading the training area with interrupting messages. Trainees can also plan ahead for using recess times for telephone messages. Outside the training area you can also set up a bulletin board where messages can be left for trainees to retrieve during recess.

Mobile Devices. State from the beginning that the use of cell phones and similar gadgets will not be allowed in the training area. That should include voice and text messaging. Allowing participants to set mobile devices to vibrate mode still alerts them to an incoming message, with the subsequent temptation to check it: this will also interrupt you and whatever activity is taking place.

Challenging Personalities. These interruptions usually come in the form of the clown (or entertainer), the loud-mouth and the monopolizer. Naturally, the categories are not mutually exclusive.

• *Clowns.* You assumed they were all adults, but you were wrong. The clown, when managed, can add humor to situations that could otherwise be dull. When left to their own devices, clowns can ruin your presentation through practical jokes, intimidating or threatening comments, or irrelevant observations that prevent participation and interrupt you. After the third attempt to tolerate the focus of your presentation, acknowledge that they have left their mark by saying:

> "Thank you for your comments, Hil. We do have quite a bit of material to cover here, and the more interruptions we get, the longer the training pro-

gram will have to go. So let's try to limit comments to questions or observations relevant to the subject here."

• *Loud-mouths*. These are people who don't know how to raise their hand or wait their turn when someone else is talking, sometimes they are just people who have to carry on their private conversations whenever someone else needs or appreciates their attention. Consider that, if you detect that the loud-mouth might actually be an expert on the subject matter, you can always find ways to enlist and engage him/her in demonstrations and explanations. This recognizes the loud-mouth and channels his/her energy productively. Depending on the situation, you can say:

> "Please, let's wait until Anna is done, then you'll have an opportunity to contribute. Thanks. Continue, Anna."

> "Milton, Mary is asking about [x, y and z]. Do you have any suggestions regarding her question?"

> "I will be done in a minute here, Doris, and then you'll have a chance to share with us all your observations. Can they wait until then?"

• *Monopolizers*. The monopolizer can be an expert who is out to show you how much he or she knows. As with the loud-mouth, you can find means to engage him/her advantageously in the training by involving the monopolizer in demonstrations, aiding others or for brief experiential narratives. However, this person can also be someone in need of attention, and wants to use your training program as a forum for concerns that may or may not be relevant to what you are doing. Sometimes the monopolizer just needs to be acknowledged. Once you have decided you cannot allow this free flow and loud philosophizing, you can address it with statements such as:

> "Charlie, since our time today is limited, I'm wondering whether we couldn't defer your considerations until the end of the day."

> "Helen, if I hear you correctly you are saying that... [paraphrase]. That certainly is a topic we could discuss for hours. Thank you for sharing those observations with us. We were saying before that the stages..."

Such statements usually acknowledge the monopolizer and allow you to go on with your presentation.

When Tact Fails. Some people don't respond to subtlety. Others are used to being told by presenters, teachers and supervisors that they are less than pleasant, and they have become immune to reprimands; still others have gotten away with it before and just don't care as long as they have their way. If you are dealing with someone like that, you can also wait until you can see them privately and tell them firmly and clearly that their behavior is undesirable and unwelcome.

You can either leave their decision to continue in the program up to them (until it becomes intolerable) or suggest that they cease to attend

"Gee, Horace, you seem to know all of the material already, judging by your comments today. Do you think you really ought to be here, wasting your time?"

"Zoe, I feel uncomfortable with the comments you have been making today. It is becoming disruptive to what we are doing. I'd prefer that you either limit your interventions or stop coming to the sessions."

Your Presentation

Presentations you make with an instructional intent have specific features: an opening that orients the learner, an exposition through which you try to maintain attention and communication, and a closure. An evaluation or application activity usually follows the presentation, or it can be immersed in the presentation and conducted at logical points. This subsection addresses each of those parts.

Orienting the Trainee. Orientation consists of statements and activities meant to relate your trainees' experience to the objectives of the training component. It puts trainees in a receptive frame of mind and focuses their attention on the content of the training component. It is meant to stimulate interest and involvement. By orienting the trainees you also create an organizing framework, a structure for ideas that are to follow (see examples on the next page).

Maintaining Interest. You can maintain interest in your presentation by retaining the attention that you capture during orientation. However, the key to maintaining interest is to vary the way in

70

Orienting Guides

Goals:
- Focus trainees' attention on the content.
- Stimulate interest.
- Provide structure.

Examples:

Are you all familiar with fishing? What happens when you have the wrong bait for the type of fish that's most abundant in those waters? That's similar to what happens with certain incentives at work.

Think for a moment about a time when you felt you were completely alone in the world, and had to start thinking in terms of doing everything for and by yourself. Have you ever had such an experience? Usually that's the feeling that personnel who conduct training in this particular part of the world feel. Let's consider why.

Beginning the process at this point is similar to starting to assemble an automobile by working around the seats. What's the most important part of a car? What happens if you develop everything around the seats instead of the engine? What are you saying about your priorities? Let's think of this process in those terms.

which you present the content. You can vary movement, sound and visual impressions.

Move. Move slowly and deliberately from right to left and from left to right in front of the room as you make an oral presentation. Small steps are all you require: sometimes just shifting the weight of your body from one side to the other is enough, particularly when coordinated with subtle changes in body and head direction. Move also from front to back of the room and among trainees. However, avoid jerky or nervous movements and don't race around the room: the idea is to engage the attention of trainees, and those sudden movements irritate to the point of achieving the opposite of what you are after.

Focus. In this context, maintaining focus refers to intentionally controlling the direction of your trainees' attention. You can achieve this through statements, by gestures or by combinations of both. (See examples of focusing tools on the opposite page.)

Shift interaction patterns. Your basic interaction patterns are trainer-group, trainer-trainee and trainee-trainee. Delivering lectures and making presentations are primarily trainer-group; individual question and answer periods and observation during practice are usually trainer-trainee. Asking probing and comprehension-check questions helps trainees remain alert, and prods them to follow your presentation. Group and teamwork usually entails trainee-trainee interaction.

Use silence. Training presenters often fear silence. Many of us learn to use talking as a defense

---

TO HELP YOU MAINTAIN ATTENTION

• Limit your talking time. Don't talk too much, nor allow others to do so either.
• Keep trainees from tuning out: use analogies and examples from fields of interest to them, and remind them of how topics interrelate.
• Use comfortable, supportive surroundings.
• Define terms and explain jargon.

◆

Examples of Focusing		
Verbal	Gestural	Combinations
Look at this chart.	Use a pointer to highlight an object.	Point to the chart and say, "Look at this chart."
Listen carefully to the next two points.	Turn your body toward an object.	Cup your ear in your hand and say, "Listen carefully to the next two points."
This issue is *extremely* important.	Use hands in conjunction with actions you describe.	Tap on the flip chart as you point to statements such as "This issue is extremely important."
Watch closely what happens when I pull the string.	Raise your eyebrows. Smile. Frown.	Make a fist and tap your belly with it has you say, "This conclusion came mostly from a gut feeling."

and forget to use it as a communication medium. However, silence can be a very effective means to capture and maintain attention. It can also serve as a transition to another topic. Silence provides time to think; it captures attention by pointing to the contrast between noise and silence, and arouses expectations. Silence also keeps you from controlling a discussion.

Help Trainees Understand

Trainers need to be constantly aware of the need to verify learner understanding. Comprehension is an excellent portal to retention: we cannot remember what we did not understand in the first place. Here are some practical ways to help participants understand.

Your Ideas Become Clearer When You:

- Use words everyone in the group can understand. When you practice your presentation, have someone other than a trainee listen to your presentation. Have that person keep track of the words that were difficult to understand. Then you can determine which to replace or define.
- Throw one idea at a time. Learning takes place in small chunks. Don't give them more than one main idea to digest at a time. Ask probing questions to test whether or not they got the idea before you move on.
- Break up complex ideas into component simpler ones. You want to enlighten, not bore by oversimplifying or confuse by compounding needlessly.
- Build on the foundation they already have. Bring up ideas they have mastered previously, and relate them to the new concepts.
- Provide overviews at the beginning of the program and at significant points in presentations, to relate new content to the overall sequence. Use overviews as maps along the way.
- Say it, then repeat it. Vary our repetition: use different terms, analogies, examples and illustrations. Some people may not get an idea when you state it, but once you "repeat" it using a different medium, it becomes clearer.

You're Talking, But Are You Listening?

Making presentations is different from lecturing. Usually lecturers request that members of the audience defer their questions until the lecture is done. Normally, you can't do that in a training situation. You must allow for questions and provide for an environment in which anyone feels free to inquire, offer suggestions and question your presentation. Don't ever ignore a hunch that someone in your group is confused or angry from the look on a face: it will come back to haunt you, and it is much healthier to address possible confusion there and then. The secret lies in knowing how to manage interpersonal communication and how to respond to observation, all of which require good listening.

Effective training presenters must know how to display attending behavior, how to be active listeners, and how to reflect.

Attending Behavior. Attending behavior includes any action or statement meant to stimulate the trainee to make disclosures without fear of reprisals or manipulation. Settings that encourage participants to make disclosures are supportive, questioning and flexible. Examples of effective and ineffective attending behavior:

Supportive	Antagonistic
After all you've said, I can see why you'd feel frustrated too!	*I can't see why you feel frustrated. I have been very clear. You can't seem to understand.*
Questioning	**Judgmental**
Could you explain why this is particularly confusing?	*Why is it that you are the only person who finds this confusing?*
Flexible	**Controlling**
Would you like to suggest an alternative to the way we have been practicing this part of the simulation?	*If alternatives were available, we'd use them, but we have to finish this program by Wednesday.*

You can show effective attending behavior by using verbal and nonverbal clues. Some clues are more effective than others, as the following examples illustrate.

Effective Nonverbal Clues	Not as effective nonverbal clues:
Eye contact that focuses on the speaker.	No eye contact or focusing on other events in the surrounding area.
Empathetic facial expressions that show you are trying to put yourself in the other person's place, to understand their situation better.	Facial expressions that show lack of concern or that show pity or patronizing attitudes.
Relaxed body posture. Comfortable allowance for personal space.	Tense body posture. Excessive physical distance from or closeness to the other person.
Effective Verbal Clues	**Not as Effective Verbal Clues**
Silence.	Constant chatter and picking on the other person's cues to start talking about your own experiences.
Brief acknowledgments.	Long silent voids that make the other person wonder whether you are listening at all.
Brief paraphrases that show understanding.	Attempts at paraphrases that actually show you weren't listening at all or putting words in the other person's mouth.

Active Listening. When you listen actively, you are showing the other person that you are listening to his or her thoughts and feelings. It means that you defer judging or criticizing the speaker in favor of showing that you are completely and accurately involved with what the person is saying and feeling. Active listening acknowledges that messages have an intellectual content and an emotional content, and that you, as the listener, are interested in understanding both.

Active Listening Examples of statements and their content		
What the speaker says:	**What the words mean:**	**What the words express:**
"I don't want help from you. I'm old enough to handle this."	I can do this by myself.	I feel independent... annoyed... irritated... humiliated...
"I've tried this six times and it still doesn't come out right."	I can't do it. I don't know how to do it.	I am frustrated... confused... angry... tired...
I can't believe this! A perfect score on the first attempt!"	I passed. I'm good at this.	I feel surprised... proud... happy... relieved...
"Your model is good on paper, but it won't work in an organization like ours."	I don't believe you. I want you to prove its worth. I don't want anything to change."	I feel skeptical... frustrated... manipulated... pressured...

Once you have listened actively to a message, you can summarize, describe, infer and interpret what the other person is saying.

Active listening requires patience. It is an activity that you cannot learn unless you are truly committed and motivated to develop the skill. When you fake active listening, you come across as patronizing or insincere.

Active listening:

- Blocks out other interfering stimuli.
- Focuses on the verbal and nonverbal messages of the speaker.
- Makes a distinction between words and emotion.
- Makes inferences about the feelings that the speaker experiences.

Reflecting. Reflecting picks up on a person's words and tires to reflect (bounce) back the gist of the message. When you reflect, you respond to the speaker's nonverbal clues by describing the speaker's actions.

Reflecting consists of:

> • *Paraphrasing*. Picking up on the speaker's words and trying to summarize them in your own words. You paraphrase when you repeat the essence of the speaker's words. This helps you initiate dialogue and motivates the speaker to provide additional information. It also gives you lead time to decide whether you want to continue the dialogue. A typical paraphrasing statement could start with, "I heard you say..." or "Let me see whether I heard you correctly."

> • *Describing behavior*. Responding to the speaker's nonverbal clues by describing the speaker's actions. When you describe, you refer only to visible evidence from the speaker's behavior. By using such a description, you give the speaker insight into how

he or she is coming across. You could begin reflecting through description by saying, "I saw that you..."

• *Inferring*: Making inferences about the emotions that the speaker is transmitting, and sharing the inference with the speaker. Inferring does not put words in the other person's mouth. When you make inferences you are trying to check out perception, without trying to second-guess the speaker's intentions. Part of inferring is clarifying to make sure that your observations are correct. Common inferring statements are, "If I were you, I imagine I'd feel... Is that how you feel about that?" "Let me see whether I understood correctly. You said that... Is this accurate?"

Closure

When you finish a major component in the training presentation, signal closure through an appropriate action or statement. Closure is meant to bring presentations to a conclusion. When you use closure techniques, you:

- Bring ideas together in the trainees' minds by consolidating major points,

- Put major components in a sequential context in the training program.

- Provide transition by linking the topic you are closing to the next topic in the sequence.

- Draw attention to the end of the major component.

Two common categories of closure are review and transfer:

Closure Categories	Features	Examples
Review	Draws trainees' attention to the end of a major segment. Reviews the main points of a presentation Relates major segments to the learning sequence in the training program.	Before moving on to the next topic, let's go over what we have seen so far, and how this topic relates to what we will be doing next. I'd like some of you to point out what you consider the main points under this topic
Transfer	Draws trainee attention to the end of a major segment. Affords trainees opportunities to practice what they have learned.	You did a great job completing the organizational audit form. Now let's turn to the summary of national trends and compare your results with those of similar organizations. Do you find significant differences?

You can hold closure activities at the close of a discussion (to summarize, for instance, or structure the main ideas produced in the discussion), to follow a film, at the end of a question-answer period, or at the end of an individual or group practice session.

Did They Learn Anything from the Presentation?

Somewhere along the line you will need to guide trainees to evaluate how their knowledge has changed by participating in your presentation. Traditionally, this is known as testing. However, more than testing, evaluation is a means for you to determine which topics may still need clarification or whether trainees are ready to move on to another component. For trainees, it provides opportunities for reward, and also for feedback regarding their performance. In the best of cases, testing helps trainees reinforce their learning by helping them review and structure their knowledge.

Although you can give trainees a pencil and a sheet of paper to write answers, you may be able to use other means to get trainees to evaluate their learning from a presentation. These approaches also help you evaluate the effectiveness of your training presentation. To do this, you should be able to use different types of questions, depending on the kind of information you want to get, and according to the types of skills you want trainees to develop.

Questions asked primarily for testing trainees on presentations can be grouped under six major headings: knowledge, comprehension, application, analysis, synthesis and evaluation.

- Knowledge questions ask trainees to recall; only memory is involved.

- Comprehension questions check understanding.

- Application questions encourage trainees to apply a rule to solve a one-answer problem.

- Analysis questions require trainees to identify reasons for a process, to break down information so that they can reach conclusions or formulate generalizations, or to find evidence that supports an idea.

- Synthesis questions encourage trainees to perform original thinking and make predictions, and to solve problems for which no single correct answer may be appropriate.

- Evaluation questions make trainees apply their knowledge in situations for which a single answer may not exist. Trainees have to judge the merit of an idea or approach as one solution to a problem. Evaluation questions include opinion.

Examples of each of these types of questions follow.

KNOWLEDGE Ask questions such as: "Define the term 'process'." "List four aspects...." "Mention the four steps..." "Name the moving parts of..." "What is a conditioned response?"

COMPREHENSION "Describe the four steps..." "Place each stage in sequential order..." "Explain each element in your own words..." "Compare..." "Rephrase..."

APPLICATION "Apply the X theorem to the following situation..." "Choose the two that meet requirements for..." "Write an example of..." "Solve..." "Use column 3 of the table to look up..." "Which belong in category TP?"

ANALYSIS "Now that the exercise is complete, what elements contributed to the results you obtained?" "This sociologist suggests that several new forces are operating in this situation. According to the comparative profile you have seen here, how can you describe those new forces? "Infer three principles of interpersonal communication from your observation of the team."

SYNTHESIS "Given these features of a task-oriented group, what results would you anticipate?" "Develop two procedures that enable your workers to bypass a production bottleneck in station 4." "Produce a model on the basis of this data..." "Combine data from both experiments to develop a hypothesis of repeated..." "Draw engine AB-2 and label its moving parts."

EVALUATION "Argue that theory A is superior to B..." "Decide which of these two procedures is more advantageous for process X..." "Judge..." "Propose at least one reason why you believe that this process should replace current practices..." "What aspects of the assessment do you consider most valuable? State your reasons."

Asking a Question: An Elusive Art

Questioning is a powerful tool. You can use it regardless of the training method you follow, and it can tell you a lot about trainee comprehension or interests. Asking effective questions goes beyond using questions that require only the call of facts. A skillful question stimulates trainees to make use of information, organize facts and draw conclusions.

Regardless of the purpose of the question, ask questions that:

• Trainees can understand clearly and unambiguously, without overloading participant concentration.

Example:
Good: *Can you name two factors that contribute to this result?*
Bad: *Is this concept important? Give me an example or two of an event or occurrence that could take place either in the laboratory or in the assembly line and, when it happens, what are the possible consequences for safety and productivity."*

• Are related to the main concepts in a presentation.

Example:
Good: *How does this topic relate to the sequence of steps we have considered so far?*
Bad: *What topic is introduced on page 21?*

To ask questions:

1. Ask the question from the group. Above all, don't call on someone and then pose the question. If the person doesn't know the answer, all you will get is embarrassment and wasted time. "Asking "pop" questions is a poor way to maintain attention, but it's an unfortunate, sure-fire way of humiliating adult learners.

2. Pause while trainees are considering a reply. Most people are either thinking of an answer

or hoping someone else has one. Give them time either way.

3. Call on a participant.

4. Listen to the response; if inappropriate or inadequate, encourage clarification from other participants. If the answer is incorrect, acknowledge it as such without calling names or putting the person down: "I don't think that this is a solution I'd apply. Anybody else?" "Think back to the issues we discussed this morning. Any other suggestions?"

If You Want to Learn More

1. Ora A. Spaid, Chapter 15, "Deliver," in *The Consummate Trainer: A Practitioner's Perspective* (Englewood Cliffs, NJ: Prentice-Hall, 1986).

2. Dugan Laird, Chapter 11, "How Important Is Teaching Technique?" in *Approaches to Training and Development*, Second Edition (Reading, MA: Addison-Wesley 1985).

3. Madelyn Burley-Allen, *Listening: The Forgotten Skill* (San Francisco: Wiley 1995).

4. William J. Rothwell, *Adult Learning Basics* (Alexandria, VA: American Society for Training and Development, 2008).

5. Raymond J. Wlodkowsky, *Enhancing Adult Motivation to Learn: A Comprehensive Guide for Teaching All Adults*, Third Edition (San Francisco: Jossey-Bass, 2007).

6. Robert Marzano, *Classroom Management That Works: Research-Based Strategies for Every Teacher* (Alexandria, VA: Association for Supervision and Curriculum Development, 2008).

7. Jane Vella, *Learning to Listen, Learning to Teach: The Power of Dialogue in Educating Adults* (San Francisco: Jossey-Bass, 2002).

8. Jon Saphier, Mary Ann Haley-Speca and Robert Gower, *The Skillful Teacher: Building*

Your Teaching Skills, Sixth Edition (Acton, MA: Research for Better Teaching, 2008).

9. Philip G. Jones, ed., Section 1, "In the Classroom: Issues, Ideas, Tips, Tricks," in *Adult Learning in Your Classroom* (Minneapolis, MN: Lakewood Books, 1982).

10. Jack J. Phillips and Patricia P. Phillips, *Beyond Learning Objectives* (Alexandria, VA: American Society for Training and Development, 2008).

11. Ruth C. Clark, *Developing Technical Training: A Structured Approach for Developing Classroom and Computer-Based Instructional Materials,* Third Edition (San Francisco: Pfeiffer, 2007).

12. Paul Hare, Edgar F. Borgatta and Robert F. Bales, *Small Groups: Studies in Social Interaction* (Oxford: Alfred A. Knopf, 1965).

13. Peter H. Martorella, Chapter 7, "Teaching Concepts," in James M. Cooper, et al., *Classroom Teaching Skills: A Handbook* (Lexington, MA: D C Heath, 1990).

14. Robert M. Bramson, "Bulldozers and Balloons," in *Coping with Difficult People* (New York: Ballantine Books, 1988).

CHAPTER 6

BEYOND THE PRESENTATION: APPLICATION TECHNIQUES

How can you help participants apply what they have learned during a presentation? One possibility is to wait until they return to the work environment. However, it is much more effective to provide learning experiences for them to try their hand at what you have told them they should be able to do.

If you are using guided discussion, demonstration and performance, or laboratory or problem solving training methods, you will very likely have to use application techniques. In training the most commonly used techniques are work exercises, case study, role playing and critiques following demonstration of skills.

Work Exercises

- Encourage participants to apply learning to a simple situation.
- Can be in the trainees' manuals or handed out when appropriate.
- Can be completed individually or in groups. Individual exercises, if too long, can reduce interest and produce prolonged periods of silence, which you may or may not desire.
- Must be representative of the contents in a presentation or reading. You are trying to make them apply information, not learn new items.

Case Studies

- Allow trainees to apply knowledge by examining a situation similar to a real-life problem.

- Promote participation in discussion following team work in analyzing a case.
- Encourage trainee involvement in the training process.
- Foster an environment in which trainees can contribute their own past experiences in problem solving and application of principles.
- Provide a structure around which trainees can develop their own ideas.
- Requires previous development of a good case study: is one that focuses on specific principles and relevant ideas against which to apply learning, and yet is realistic enough for trainees.

Role Playing

- Can focus on individuals who make presentations to the whole group, or can be a small-group activity.
- Requires that the role be specific, and that guidelines for the role be provided to all participants in the activity.
- Sometimes causes hesitation and resistance from participants. Resistance grows in relation to the lack of belief in the activity.
- Is enhanced by videotaping and a subsequent group critique.

Critiques

- Usually follow role playing or skill demonstrations by trainees.
- Should be meant to provide coaching assistance and feedback regarding performance. (The next section summarizes the characteristics of good feedback.)

- Are meant to be a reinforcement and retraining tool: trainees need to know how they are doing, and good critiques are good feedback.
- Emphasize rewards for improved performance instead of punishment for specific deficiencies.
- Accentuate the positive by focusing on the relative weight of positive comments against the negative. This doesn't mean that weaknesses are overlooked. It does mean that the negative can be expressed in positive terms. "This is an important step, Sydney, because the whole structure could collapse if you don't bolt it right. For that reason, make sure the next time you turn the bolt counterclockwise." (To replace, "You bolted that wrong again, Sydney. Do it right the next time.")
- Select aspects of importance and overlook minor flaws in application or demonstration. Over-stressing the negative erodes self-confidence.
- Uses praise without patronizing or embarrassing. "That's right, Susan, you have done it correctly. Congratulations! I particularly liked the way you concentrated on eye contact this time."
- Encourage other participants to become involved, following a specific model. You, for instance, can set guidelines for critiques, by requesting others to contribute: "Two aspects of Mortimer's presentation you thought were particularly outstanding... Two aspects you would have approached differently."

Feedback

Why feedback? Feedback helps others change their own behavior. Feedback gives people information about how their behavior influences others, or how they are performing a task. It keeps people's behavior focused on better ways to achieve goals. Feedback is generally more useful if it:

- Describes: it reports the facts, not your own ideas about why something happened.
- Specifies: it focuses on a specific instance of behavior, rather than addressing general issues that make the receiver defensive.
- Takes into account the receiver's readiness for feedback.
- Takes timing into account: the closer the feedback is to the moment when the event took place, the better. However, critical feedback in front of others may be damaging, even if it is given shortly after the event took place.
- Focuses on a few items at a time: running down a list of items makes the receiver shut down or become defensive.
- Means to help: destructive comments serve only the aggressive needs of the person giving the feedback, and disregard the needs of the person receiving it.
- Checks the person giving the feedback checks with the receiver by asking for paraphrases or reflection (see Chapter 5) to make sure that they receiver's understanding of the feedback matches the intended message.

If You Want to Learn More

1. Ora A. Spaid, Chapter 10, "The Content Finders-Keepers Process," in *The Consummate Trainer: A Practitioner's Perspective* (Englewood Cliffs, NJ: Prentice-Hall, 1977).

2. John Hansen, Chapter 9, "Observation Skills," in James M. Cooper, et al., *Classroom Teaching Skills: A Handbook* (Lexington, MA: D C Heath, 1990).

3. Terry Tenbrink, Chapter 10, "Evaluation," in James M. Cooper, et al., *Classroom Teaching Skills: A Handbook* (Lexington, MA: D C Heath, 1990).

4. Dugan Laird, Chapter 16, "How Do You Evaluate Training and Development?" in *Approaches to Training and Development*, Second Edition (Reading, MA: Addison-Wesley, 1982).

5. William J. Kryspin and John F. Feldhusen, Developing Classroom Tests: *A Guide for Writing and Evaluating Test Items* (Minneapolis, MN: Burgess Publishing Co., 1970).

6. Gilbert Sax, *Principles of Educational and Psychological Measurement and Evaluation* (Belmont, CA: Wadsworth, 1996).

7. Albert Oosterhof, *Developing and Using Classroom Assessments*, Fourth Edition (New York: Pearson, 2008).

8. William J. Rothwell, *Adult Learning Basics* (Alexandria, VA: American Society for Training and Development, 2008).

9. Rosemary S. Caffarella *Planning programs for adult learners: a practical guide for Educators, Trainers, and Staff Developers*, Second Edition (San Francisco: Jossey-Bass, 2010).

10. Sharon B. Merriam, Rosemary S. Caffarella and Lisa M. Baumgartner, *Learning in Adulthood: A Comprehensive Guide* (San Francisco: Jossey-Bass, 2007).

11. Robert Marzano, *Classroom Management That Works: Research-Based Strategies for Every Teacher* (Alexandria, VA: Association for Supervision and Curriculum Development, 2008).

12. Jon Saphier, Mary Ann Haley-Speca and Robert Gower, *The Skillful Teacher: Building Your Teaching Skills,* Sixth Edition (Acton, MA: Research for Better Teaching, 2008).

13. Jackie A. Walsh, Elizabeth D. Satter, *Quality Questioning: Research-Based Practice to Engage Every Learner* (London: Sage, 2004).

14. Jack J. Phillips and Patricia P. Phillips, *Beyond Learning Objectives* (Alexandria, VA: American Society for Training and Development, 2008).

15. Angus Reynolds and Thomas Iwinski, *Multimedia Training: Developing Technology-*

Based Systems (New York: McGraw-Hill, 1996).

CHAPTER 7

USEFUL TOOLS:
VISUALS AND HANDOUTS

"A picture is worth a thousand words." No one ever bothered to explain that the thousand words can become quite offensive, especially when trainers forget certain principles or visual communication. Likewise, handouts can be fountains of information or puddles of irritation. It all depends on how you handle them in training.

Reminders for Visual Communication

In training, the use of visual resources implies that the visual images and text are compatible. It also requires that you remember issues of simplicity, legibility and consistency. The pages that follow zero in on specific recommendations for preparing visuals and for evaluating resources you may need to use.

Correspondence between Words and Images. What you say and what trainees see should be mutually supportive, not conflicting.

- Use visuals as starting points or as illustrations of verbal content, but don't read them word for word. Remember that most of your trainees can read, and faster than you can repeat words form an overhead transparency or a PowerPoint slideshow online.

- When done with an overhead projector or large screen, shut it off: don't leave the light image shining on the wall, taking the trainees' attention away from what you are saying.

- Talk to trainees, not to the screen or projection on the wall. If you are using an overhead projector or a computer-generated projection and need to refer to the content on the visual, look at it on the projector itself.

- When using projected images (transparencies, slides, computer-generated or compact-disc visuals), point to items on the image itself. Most computer-based presentation software includes online pointers or stylus-controlled drawing tools you can control with a mouse or touch-screen technology.

- Write on the chalkboard, flip chart or overhead acetate as you develop the presentation. Use colored chalk and markers, especially if you wish to establish contrasts.

- Use the pause control for audio tapes, video discs and film to stop for comments as appropriate.

- Show only the useful segments of video media.

- Provide a background that explains why you are showing a visual, and direct trainees to look for an idea, image or situation if a visual cannot isolate items.

- Show what is being talked about. Avoid selecting video media that show "talking heads." Most trainers, through direct explanation, can do a better job than a static, totally untalented speaker on video, even if the subject is a world-renowned expert on the topic. If motion media does not demonstrate what it describes, it is usually dull. Training department shelves are overstacked with examples to support this claim.

- Watch trainees and pick up on nonverbal clues that indicate how they are reacting to your visual presentation; restructure accordingly.

Unacceptable:

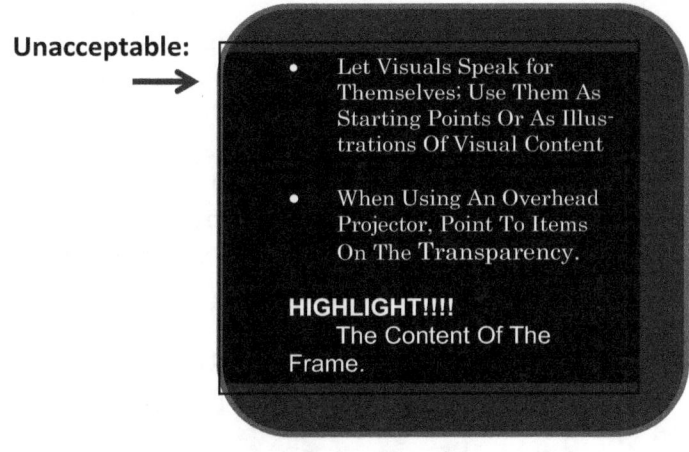

Improved

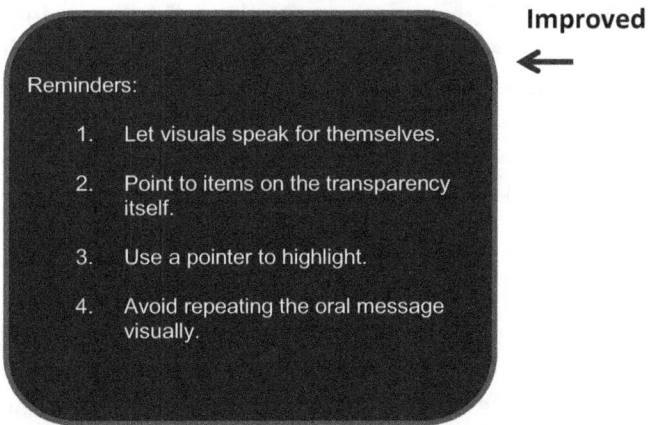

Simplicity and Impact. Visual resources should clarify key ideas, and help trainees link important pieces of information. Visuals, therefore, should be concise, but not so telegraphic that their meaning is lost.

Don't use visuals for the sake of ornament. If they are not communicating something, skip them. Likewise, they should not communicate any more than the point you are trying to make.

- Make the visual message big (within reason, preventing distortion and visual overload) and keep it simple.

- Have a focus: if you want to highlight a concept, isolate the concept by presenting it alone or by using color, lines, or a different font style (bold, for example).

- To emphasize or direct attention, use key words instead of whole paragraphs.

- Number or bullet key points.

- Sans serif fonts are generally much more legible than serif: E is an example of sans serif (no twists on terminals), while **E** is serif.

- Use color, but use it selectively and to focus attention on something. Never use red, blue or green backgrounds for black lettering on overhead slides.

- Computer-based presentation systems currently offer developers of visual materials a broader range of easy-to-use palettes. Use your judgment when you select color combinations: what seems "interesting" to you may interfere with readability.

- Use visual contrast by varying color, white space and type size. However, don't mix fonts within information groups on a visual.

- Avoid intricate illustrations and graphics with excessive detail.

- Normally, limit lines of text on visuals to about six lines per frame, and about six words per line; this varies with type size and distance from which trainees may need to see your visual.

- Provide handouts with copies of important visuals, such as illustrations, diagrams and charts.

Consistency. The visuals you use for training purposes should transmit content accurately. Their style should be appropriate to trainees' educational and age levels.

- Be consistent in visual elements and style to reduce the possibility of confusion.

- Use charts and graphs where useful to illustrate patterns and clarify concepts.

- Verify that related data are consistent in presentation and content throughout visuals.

Handouts
Yes, handouts are often necessary. They are useful as supplements to training content, to summarize points, and to provide direction in exercises.

Following presentations and practice, they can also detail procedures and reminders that the trainee can use as job aids.

However, consider the amount of handouts you plan to distribute during a training session. Too many handouts tend to disorient trainees: they become something else to manage, rather than a source of information. You may want to consider binding them as a separate unit and then refer to them as required in training.

Another issue to consider regarding handouts is when to distribute them. Handouts can be helpful reminders for closure and transition. Make sure you distribute them when you need them, and not before.

Finally, trainees are generally unimpressed with handouts that sound like afterthoughts. The message seems to be that you were not prepared. If the information is important and relevant enough to include in the training program, look for a place for handouts at appropriate places in other training materials.

If You Want to Learn More

1. Dugan Laird, Chapter 13, "What About Visual Aids?" in *Approaches to Training and Development*, Second Edition (Reading, MA: Addison-Wesley, 1985).

2. Ruth C. Clark, *Developing Technical Training: A Structured Approach for Developing Classroom and Computer-Based Instructional Materials*, Third Edition (San Francisco: Pfeiffer, 2007)

3. Robert Heinich, Michael Molenda and James D. Russell, *Instructional Media and the New Technologies of Instruction* (New York: John Wiley & Sons, 1988).

4. Angus Reynolds, Thomas Iwinski, *Multimedia Training: Developing Technology-Based Systems* (New York: McGraw-Hill, 1996).

5. Leslie Kelly, *The ASTD Handbook for Technical and Skills Training* (Alexandria, VA: American Society for Training and Development, 1994).

6. Martin M. Broadwell, "The Use and Misuse of A-V," *Training*, October 1970, p. 40.

7. Larry Samovar and Jack Mills, Chapter 1, Section 3, "Sound and Action—Presenting the Message," in *Oral Communication: Message and Response* (Dubuque, IA: Wm. C. Brown Co. Publishers, 1976).

8. Carol E. Kasworm, Amy D. Rose and Jovita M. Ross-Gordon, *Handbook of Adult and Continuing* Education (London, Sage, 2010).

9. Alan Jay Zaremba, *Organizational Communication*, Sixth Edition (New York: Oxford University Press, 2009).

10. Albert C. Book and C. Dennis Schlick, Chapter 11, "Typography," in *Fundamentals of Copy and Layout* (Lincolnwood, IL: NTC Business Books, 1996).

11. Steven Davis, *Color Perception: Philosophical, Psychological, Artistic and Computational* (New York: Oxford University Press, 2000).

CHAPTER 8

WHO'S MINDING THE GROUP?

Unless you are tutoring or coaching one individual, the training you provide is directed at groups. Sometimes you need to address the whole group. However, some training activities are better suited to small group arrangements. You should be familiar with managing group activities, your role in the training group, group size concerns, and strategies for getting groups going. It is also helpful to be able to identify an effective group.

Managing a Group Activity

The steps involved in managing a training group activity include stating the purpose, providing guidance, forming groups, monitoring the groups, reassembling the groups and wrapping up the activity.

1. *State the purpose*. When you announce the activity, tell participants what they are about to do and what their goal is.

2. *Provide guidance*. Tell them what they will be doing, step by step. If you have directions on handouts, tell them the major steps while you have their full attention, before you give them handouts to read. If group members will have roles to play in the individual groups, such as leader or recorder, tell them what the roles are, so that they can start thinking about which they prefer to play. Also, alert the group to time limits and tell them that you will be reminding them of time availability as they proceed. While you give direction and instruction, point out materials they may

want to use for recording or for preparing to report back to the larger group. If they are going to use props or equipment, they need to know where those are.

3. *Form groups.* How many groups you form depends on how much time and how many participants you have. It also depends on your own role in the group: if you are going to facilitate or lead discussion, you have to decide how you will manage your own participation depending on the number of groups. Some trainers have assistants who monitor or facilitate group work; this also adds another dimension to the management function. Remember that if you want groups to be able to report back at the end of the session, you must have enough time to let all group representatives make presentations.

The number of groups also depends on the training room's layout and availability of space, as well as how rooms are configured for break-out sessions. If group profile is important, prepare a list of group members beforehand and simply assign participants to a group. Otherwise, you can form groups by counting off (1-2-3, then the next person starts with 1 again; all the 1s form a group, all the 2s another, and so forth). You can also have people draw colored markers from a bag.

4. *Monitor groups.* It is extremely important that you remain in the room at all times during group activities. You must be available for consultation, and you have to carry out timekeeping activities. Your absence is a clear indication that you are not serious about the activity. Listen carefully to groups as you walk around the room, because they may need further direction and instructions. This also provides you information about their work, so that you can give groups feedback about content and process at the end of the activity.

5. *Reassemble the groups.* Indicate the order in which reports will begin from each group, or request volunteers to start, if order is not important. As each group reports, you may want to request that others comment about the report.

6. *Wrap up the activity.* Let participants know that the activity is over by restating the purpose of the activity, summarizing the main points that the groups presented, asking for additional comments and thanking participants.

Trainer Involvement in Group Activities

How involved you get in group activities depends on why you put the group together in the first place. Training groups are usually assembled as task, discussion or discovery groups.

Task Groups

Participants: Have a specific task to accomplish: listing steps in a process, assembling a tool, analyzing a case.

Trainer: Is outside the group, avoiding interference; monitors activity to ensure that participants understand the task and have the materials they need.

Discussion Groups

Participants: Discuss openly topics of importance to the training program, often follow a task-group activity or presentation, and serves as a medium for synthesis of knowledge or as a means for closure.

Trainer: Listens and coordinates; can adjust participation by directing traffic, acknowledging participants, and pointing to time constraints. The trainer has to be sensitive to when enough discussion has taken place, and indicate that the next participant will be the last, or that following the next participant the group will start summarizing. In this role, the trainer may also be a facilitator, making sure that all participants' contributions are respected and that the discussion is limited to issues, not personalities.

Discovery Groups

Participants: Focus on a problem that is generally stated as "What can we do to...?"Participants make a statement about an issue or problem, and are challenged to prove their point or elaborate. All solutions come from participants, who develop skills in reaching solutions by allowing as much input as possible, and in developing commitment to action once they decide on a solution.

Trainer: Starts the group, often by providing a problem statement or scenario; listens to a statement from a participant to prove the point or explain further. "What do you mean?" "Example?" "How would you accomplish that?" The trainer encourages group members to react and continues to challenge them. After enough explanations for potential solutions are available, the trainer recedes to the background and allows the group to reach its own conclusions. No solution

115

comes from the trainer, whose main role following the challenge is to facilitate, ensuring that all solutions are listened to and considered, and keeping time.

The Right Size for You

How big should a group be? Group size depends on your goal and the nature of the activity. However, for most group activities:

If the number of participants is:	The group:
2	Is not a group: it's a conversation or a one-on-one tutorial.
3	Is the smallest group. Since generating ideas seems to be proportional to the number of people who compose the group, you cannot expect this to be the most effective group.
4	Can be an effective group. However, if you are expecting the group to produce its own ideas, you have to hope for neutral issues. These groups can produce deadlocks.
5-6	Is generally the best-sized group in terms of manageability and productivity.
7	Can be an effective group, but it is beginning to get too big for work groups.

8-9 Starts to break up into subgroups with agendas separate from that of the work group. With this many people, decision-making tends to take longer.

10+ Is unsatisfactory, unless your goal is to illustrate by action the types of problems that large groups have in analyzing problems and making decisions.

Get the Group Discussion Going!

Some time-tested strategies are available to you for starting a group discussion and keeping it going, when your role as trainer includes leading discussion.

- **Provide a topic or question.**
  This should answer the question, "What are we going to discuss?" The task must be small enough to address in the period of time that you have allocated for it. Trainees must also be clear on how the group task fits into the training objective.

- **Set rules for shared time and participation.**
  (1) Start out by going around the group.
  (2) Model the behavior first. While you model, call the group members' attention to what you are doing.
  (3) Following your model, choose a group member who almost certainly will give you the reply or suggestion that you want.

(4) Acknowledge and reward members verbally for their contribution

As Facilitator, You Get Them to Participate When You...

- State that you want it and expect it.

"I believe that these issues are best resolved when everyone's involved in the solution. I expect everyone here to contribute ideas about this problem, and that will strengthen the skills for which we are training here."

"No, I don't have a preconceived solution, and if I did I wouldn't share it with you. We need *your* ideas."

- Use verbal and nonverbal clues to indicate that you believe in their ability to solve the problem.

- Listen to understand what group members are communicating.

"Then what you are saying is..." "Is this accurate?" "Luis, could you get through that again? I'm not sure we were all able to follow you." "Could someone help us out?" "I can't quite follow Petrov. We need someone to put it in other words."

- Use contributions when appropriate.

- Be sure that you and the rest of the group understand the contribution from a member. If unclear, ask for a paraphrase or rewording.

- Link contributions to the discussion when they don't seem to fit clearly. If statements seem vague, look for a core concept that can be related to the discussion topic.

- Accept all contributions as potentially valuable until the group decides to use them or discard them.

- Inquire whether all members are aware of and clear on the point under discussion. When comments seem to be repeatedly irrelevant, take it as a clue that clarification may be necessary; restate the purpose or topic.

- Remember that acceptance does not equal agreement; participants should know that you appreciate their contribution and acknowledge their right to have an opinion, whether or not you agree with it.

- Cut off monopolizing speakers if necessary. Seek the reactions of those who tend to recede into the background and withhold opinions.

- Model communication behaviors that you want participants to follow
  - Use first names (if appropriate).
  - Maintain eye contact.
  - Listen with interest. Respond to a previous statement or question before changing the topic.
  - Ask members to clarify when you feel it is necessary. Paraphrase group member statements if you feel this would make an

idea clearer for others in the group. You can also ask other group members to clarify, and reflect on it with the original speaker.

- Demonstrate patience and genuine interest in understanding contributions from group members.
- Attend to the feelings and meanings that may be conveyed in the verbal messages of members.
- Use language that limits discussion of behavior to the group's activity at the particular session. When you need to pint out undesirable behavior: "This is the second time you bring up that issue today, Wanda, and perhaps we should discuss it now," NOT "Last Monday you also brought up that annoying issue, and maybe you want to bring it out once and for all."
- Use confrontation when appropriate to the task, or if avoiding confrontation becomes an obstacle to the progress of the group. Confrontational speech describes the behavior of the other speaker and describes your reactions to that behavior, in a constructive and assertive way, and expects feedback: "You have interrupted Mark three times already since we started, and I feel uncomfortable with it. Do you have a problem with waiting until he is finished?" NOT "You rude jerk, why don't you stop making me sick and wait your turn?"

• Establish strategies that support and encourage interaction.

120

- Call attention to member questions and statements that have not been listened to. "Sandy, Moira has an observation. Could you repeat it, Moira, please?"
- Use nonverbal clues such as eye contact and gestures to direct the discussion. For example, when you expect others to become involved in the discussion, y9ou can look around for more contributions or move your arms in ways that indicate you expect more.
- Distribute responsibility for replies or reactions among other group members when a group member requests that you contribute as leader or facilitator. You can also defer your opinion until enough discussion has taken place in the group.
- As leader, use facts respectfully. Relate your own ideas, attitudes, concepts and experience, but make sure that you label them as such, and highlight the tentative nature of your suggestions until the group has explored a subject or a solution.

- Maintain direction.
    - When the group goes off track, intervene by pointing out the need to return to the task.
    - Remind group members of the agenda and time limits when necessary. However, refrain from constant reminders of lack of time: eventually someone will wonder why they are bothering to tackle an issue when no time is available to do it, and probably suggest that they wait until enough time becomes available.

Is This Group Effective?

Task-oriented groups and work teams need to exhibit certain characteristics to show that they have developed into a productive unit. As a trainer whose roles include managing and facilitating group activities, you should be able to determine when your group has a better chance to be productive. If it does not look promising, you can try to restructure the group, use interpersonal communication skills to surface conflicts, or evaluate your approach to group management.

In an effective group:

- Members acknowledge all seriously-intended contributions.
- Members check out their understanding of a member's meaning before agreeing or disagreeing with a contribution.
- Members speak for themselves: the use of "I" prevails over "You" or "They" when expressing opinions or attributing beliefs: "I believe that...," rather than "I'm sure that others agree with me" or "People wouldn't agree with that."
- All contributions belong to the group. The group decides whether to use the contributions.
- Though members vary in approaches and opinions, all members participate in complementary ways.
- When the group detects a problem that hinders its progress, it stops and attempts to find the reason.
- Members seek to find the source of a problem without focusing on blaming selves or others for problems. The group focuses instead on taking measures to prevent a problem from happening again.
- The group brings conflict into the open and handles it by attacking issues, not personalities.
- Decisions are made openly, rather than by default: members know that a decision is expected of the group, and commit to their decisions enthusiastically through a process of consensus.

If You Want to Learn More

1. Diane Coutu, "Why Teams Don't Work," in *Harvard Business Review on Building Better Teams* (Cambridge, MA: Harvard University Press, 2011).

2. Bob Frisch, "When Teams Can't Decide," in *Harvard Business Review on Building Better Teams* (Cambridge, MA: Harvard University Press, 2011).

3. William G. Dyer, Jr., Jeffrey H. Dyer and Edgar H. Schein, *Team Building: Strategies for Improving Team Performance*, Fourth Edition (San Francisco: Jossey-Bass, 2007).

4. Sandra Sokolove, Myra Sadker and Savid Sadker, Chapter 7, "Interpersonal Communication Skills," in James M. Cooper, et al., *Classroom Teaching Skills: A Handbook* (Lexington, MA: D C Heath, 1990).

5. Joseph A. Olmstead, *Small-Group Instruction* (Alexandria, VA: Human Resources Research Organization, 1974).

6. Don Koberg and Jim Bagnall, *The All New Universal Traveler* (Los Altos, CA: William Kaufmann, Inc., 1981).

7. Allan D. Frank, Chapter 8, "Communicating in Small Groups to Solve Problems," in *Communicating on the Job* (Glenview, IL: Scott, Foresman & Co., 1982).

8. Anne Harlan and John J. Gabarro, *Note on Process Observation* (Boston, MA: Harvard Business School, 1976).

9. William L. Brembeck and William S. Howell, Chapter 7, "The Influences of Social Behavior on Persuasion," in *Persuasion: A Means of Social Influence*, Second Edition (Englewood Cliffs, NJ: Prentice-Hall, 1976).

10. Warren Bennis, "The 4 Competencies of Leadership," *Training and Development Journal*, August 1984, pp. 15-19.

11. Herbert A. Thelan, *Dynamics of Groups at Work* (Chicago: University of Chicago Press, 1963).

12. Ernest G. Bormann, *Discussion and Group Methods* (New York: McGraw-Hill, 1972).

13. Paul Hare; Edgar F. Borgatta; Robert F. Bales, *Small Groups: Studies in Social Interaction* (Oxford: Alfred A. Knopf, 1965).

14. Alan Jay Zaremba, *Organizational Communication*, Sixth Edition (New York: Oxford University Press, 2009).

15. Barbara Benedict Bunker, Billie T. Alban, *The Handbook of Large Group Methods: Creating Systemic Change in Organizations and Communities* (San Francisco: Jossey-Bass, 2006).